Craig Dobbins' Hymns for Fingerstyle Guitar

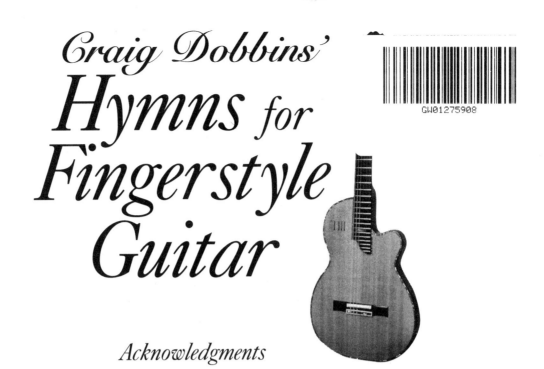

Acknowledgments

Special thanks to Clyde Kendrick, whose advice, assistance, and generosity have been invaluable to me. Special thanks also to my wife, Julie, for her encouragement and help.

This collection is dedicated to my parents, C.B. and Myrtrice Dobbins, who from childhood have instilled in me a love for these songs.

Finally, a special acknowledgement to Chet Atkins and Paul Yandell, whose great fingerstyle playing has inspired me and so many other guitarists.

—Craig Dobbins

Sand Classical Electric Guitar Courtesy of Kirk Sand
Project Manager: Aaron Stang
Technical Editor: Albert Nigro
Photography: David Moon
Cover Design: Joann Carrera

WARNER BROS. PUBLICATIONS - THE GLOBAL LEADER IN PRINT
USA: 15800 NW 48th Avenue, Miami, FL 33014

WARNER/CHAPPELL MUSIC
CANADA: 85 SCARSDALE ROAD, SUITE 101
DON MILLS, ONTARIO, M3B 2R2
SCANDINAVIA: P.O. BOX 533, VENDEVAGEN 85 B
S-182 15, DANDERYD, SWEDEN
AUSTRALIA: P.O. BOX 353
3 TALAVERA ROAD, NORTH RYDE N.S.W. 2113

NUOVA CARISCH
ITALY: VIA M.F. QUINTILIANO 40
20138 MILANO
SPAIN: MAGALLANES, 25
28015 MADRID

INTERNATIONAL MUSIC PUBLICATIONS LIMITED
ENGLAND: SOUTHEND ROAD,
WOODFORD GREEN, ESSEX IG8 8HN
FRANCE: 25 RUE DE HAUTEVILLE, 75010 PARIS
GERMANY: MARSTALLISTR. 8, D-80539 MUNCHEN
DENMARK: DANMUSIK, VOGNMAGERGADE 7
DK 1120 KOBENHAVNK

© 1997 WARNER BROS. PUBLICATIONS
All Rights Reserved

Any duplication, adaptation or arrangement of the compositions
contained in this collection requires the written consent of the Publisher.
No part of this book may be photocopied or reproduced in any way without permission.

Contents

	Page #	CD Track #
O for a Thousand Tongues to Sing	3	1
At the Cross	6	2
'Tis So Sweet to Trust in Jesus	10	3
The Old Rugged Cross	14	4
Sweet Hour of Prayer	18	5
What a Friend We Have in Jesus	21	6
Since Jesus Came into My Heart	24	7
Amazing Grace	28	8
Leaning on the Everlasting Arms	32	9
In the Garden	36	10
Jesus, Keep Me Near the Cross	40	11
There is a Fountain	44	12

O For A Thousand Tongues To Sing

*O for a thousand tongues to sing my great Redeemer's praise,
The glories of my God and King, the triumphs of His grace.*

About the music...

Charles Wesley (brother of John Wesley, founder of the Methodist movement) wrote nearly *sixty-five-hundred* hymn-poems, including *Hark! The Herald Angels Sing*. He wrote the text of this majestic hymn in 1749. It was later set to music by Carl Glaser. *O for a Thousand Tongues to Sing* is considered above all others to be the "theme song" of the Methodist church.

Performance notes...

One of my favorite arranging ideas is to begin with just the melody, gradually adding harmony with each verse, until I have built to full chords.

Measure 1 begins with the melody in single notes, leading to two-part harmony at the pickup to measure 9. Full chords begin at measure 17, with a moving bass line at measure 25. I like to imagine a massive pipe organ playing this part.

At the pickup to measure 33, it's back to single string melody, and a touch of two-part harmony again at the pickup to measure 37.

I used a classical thumb and fingers technique (although I did wear a thumbpick!).

About the recording...

I used a deep-body, Kirk Sand nylon-string electric.

O For A Thousand Tongues To Sing

Words by Charles Wesley

Music by Carl Glaser
Arranged by Craig B. Dobbins

© 1997 WARNER BROS. PUBLICATIONS U.S. INC.
All Rights Reserved

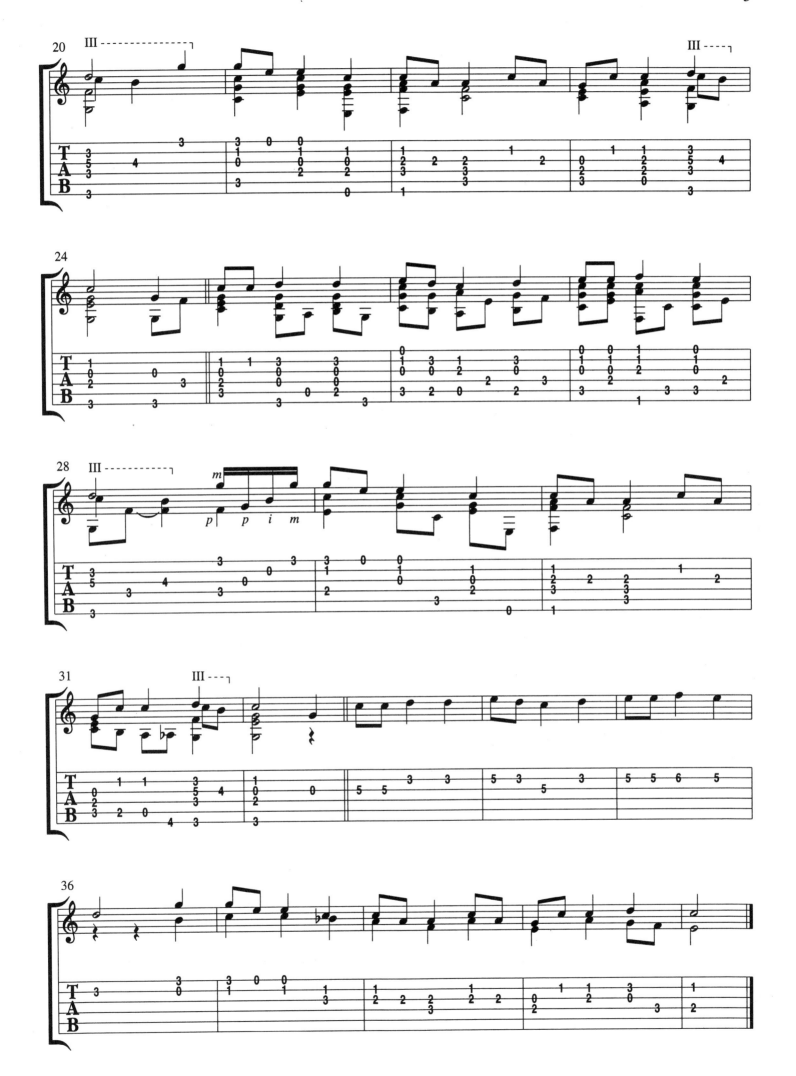

At The Cross

*At the cross, at the cross where I first saw the light,
And the burden of my heart rolled away,
It was there by faith I received my sight,
And now I am happy all the day!*

About the music...

The text to this early American hymn was written by the eighteenth century English hymnwriter Isaac Watts, probably best known as the composer of the Christmas favorite, *Joy To The World.* The original title was *Alas! And Did My Saviour Bleed?* The music (and text for the chorus) was written by Ralph E. Hudson.

Performance notes...

I play the tune once freely, and then again in alternating bass fingerstyle. Watch out for the shifts from four-four to cut time.

When you take the D.S. al Coda at measure 48, play freely from the sign through measure 15, then *a tempo* in cut time at the coda (measure 49).

About the recording...

I used the Kirk Sand nylon-string electric.

At The Cross

Words by Isaac Watts

Music by Ralph E. Hudson
Arranged by Craig B. Dobbins

'Tis So Sweet To Trust In Jesus

*Jesus, Jesus, how I trust Him! How I've proved Him o'er and o'er!
Jesus, Jesus, precious Jesus! O for grace to trust Him more!*

About the music...

The text was written by Louisa M. Stead. Professor William J. Kirkpatrick, a native of Ireland, composed the music in 1882.

Performance notes...

On the recording, I'm capoed at the 1st fret, which puts me in that great guitar key, D flat. Not to worry, though, the music is written in C.

I've used a descending bass line wherever possible, to give the tune a feeling of movement. You may also notice an occasional measure of two-four time. Other than that, the arrangement isn't that much different than one you might hear a church pianist play.

There are triplet rolls in measures 9 and 10, and a sixteenth note roll in measure 11. Consult the music for fingering.

I play the verse twice, and then the chorus twice, with slight variations each time. In measures 21 and 22, the harmony moves between the I and V chords (C and G). In measures 31 and 32, I used I - iii - IV - V (C - Em - F - G), for just a little variety.

About the recording...

Here I used a Martin steel-string acoustic, with a Thinline saddle pickup. No microphones were used. I also recorded this one *sans thumbpick*, to get a smoother sound in the bass.

'Tis So Sweet To Trust In Jesus

Words by Louisa M. Stead

Music by Wm. J. Kirkpatrick
Arranged by Craig B. Dobbins

© 1997 WARNER BROS. PUBLICATIONS U.S. INC.
All Rights Reserved

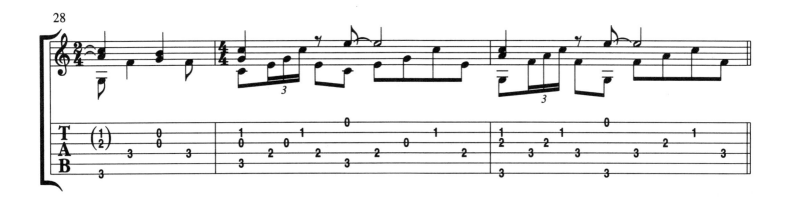

The Old Rugged Cross

So I'll cherish the old rugged cross, til my trophies at last I lay down;
I will cling to the old rugged cross, and exchange it some day for a crown.

About the music...

The Methodist evangelist George Bennard wrote this hymn in 1913. It is reported to be the most popular gospel song of the twentieth century. An interesting footnote: Rev. Bennard composed this tune *on his guitar*.

Performance notes...

The opening section of the tune is in artificial harmonics played simultaneously with regular notes, a great **Chet Atkins** technique. Touch the string 12 frets above the tab number with the tip of your right index finger and play the note with your thumb. The regular note is played by your middle or ring finger. There are also artificial harmonics in measures 27 and 58.

At measure 31, I play the melody in single notes with vibrato.

In measures 47 through 50, I use a *three finger* tremolo pattern (p, m, i) that sounds in triplets. The thumb plays the bass note, and the middle and index fingers follow with the tremolo on the melody note. Listen closely to the recording to get the idea.

About the recording...

I used the Kirk Sand nylon-string electric.

The Old Rugged Cross

Words and Music by George Bennard
Arranged by Craig B. Dobbins

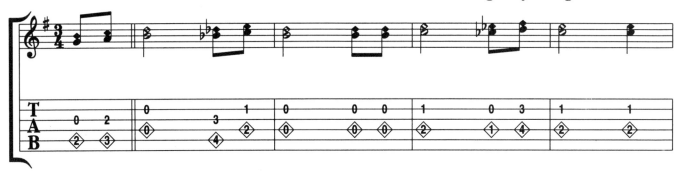

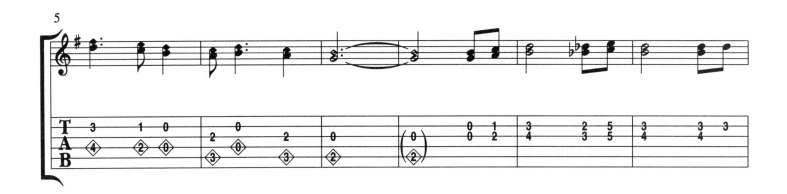

© 1997 WARNER BROS. PUBLICATIONS U.S. INC.
All Rights Reserved

16

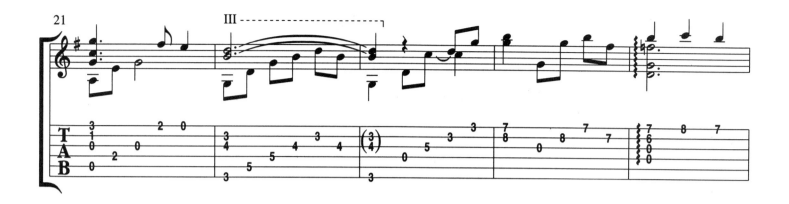

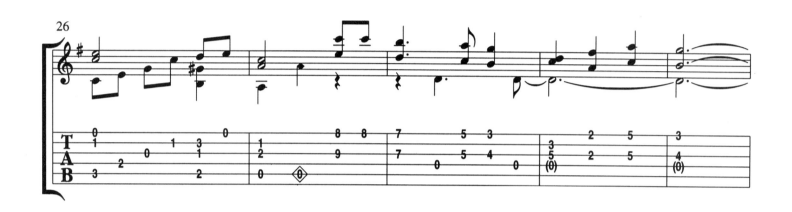

Sweet Hour Of Prayer

Words by William Walford

Music by William B. Bradbury
Arranged by Craig B. Dobbins

© 1997 WARNER BROS. PUBLICATIONS U.S. INC.
All Rights Reserved

Sweet Hour Of Prayer

*In seasons of distress and grief, My soul has often found relief
And oft escaped the tempter's snare, By thy return, sweet hour of prayer.*

About the music...

A blind preacher named William Walford wrote the text for this hymn in 1851. It was set to music by William Bradbury, who also composed the music for *Just As I Am*.

Performance notes...

When I play this tune, I picture Floyd Cramer at the piano, playing that great signature lick. I try to approximate the sound with quick hammers (see grace notes in measures 1, 8, 9 and elsewhere). I play the verse once, and the chorus twice. Play with feeling all the way through, and ritard. from measure 33 to the end. That's a hammer/pull-off combination in measure 35.

About the recording...

I used the Kirk Sand guitar.

What A Friend We Have In Jesus

*O what peace we often forfeit, O what needless pain we bear
All because we do not carry everything to God in prayer!*

About the music...

The text was written by the Canadian Joseph Scriven (an Irish immigrant) in 1855. It was later set to music by Charles C. Converse.

Performance notes...

My arrangement of *What A Friend* is somewhat jazz flavored. I left the melody alone, but I did tamper with the harmony a bit.

There's a lot of movement going on in the bass here. Check out the descending scale in measure 7, for example.

Watch out for the three finger forward roll in measure 19. That is, of course, another patented **Chet Atkins** lick.

Hold the C chord at measure 24 while you play the artificial harmonics.

About the recording...

Again, I used the Kirk Sand guitar.

What A Friend We Have In Jesus

Words by Joseph M. Scriven

Music by Charles C. Converse
Arranged by Craig B. Dobbins

© 1997 WARNER BROS. PUBLICATIONS U.S. INC.
All Rights Reserved

Since Jesus Came Into My Heart

*What a wonderful change in my life has been wrought
Since Jesus came into my heart.*

About the music...

The text was written by Rufus McDaniel, and set to music by Charles Gabriel in 1914.

Performance notes...

This arrangement mixes classical, thumbstyle and Carter-style techniques.

The full strums at the pickup to measure 1 and elsewhere should be played with your thumb. The rest of the intro is in classical thumb and fingers style.

At measure 5, it's thumbstyle! The thumb plays the downstem notes, and the fingers play the upstem notes. Remember to mute the bass strings with the palm of your right hand.

I play a verse Carter-style beginning at measure 37. Play the single notes with your thumb, and strum with your fingers (except where noted). Play the eighth note after each strum as an upstroke with your index finger.

About the recording...

I used the Martin steel-string on this tune.

Since Jesus Came Into My Heart

Words by Rufus McDaniel

Music by Charles Gabriel
Arranged by Craig B. Dobbins

© 1997 WARNER BROS. PUBLICATIONS U.S. INC.
All Rights Reserved

26

Amazing Grace

*Amazing grace! How sweet the sound, That saved a wretch like me!
I once was lost, but now am found, Was blind, but now I see.*

About the music...

Once the cruel captain of a British slave ship, John Newton went on to become an ordained Anglican minister. *Amazing Grace* is his autobiography in song. Lowell Mason arranged the early American campmeeting melody so familiar to us today.

Performance notes...

This arrangement takes you through three keys and several playing styles.

I begin with the melody in single string artificial harmonics in the key of G. At measure 15, I switch to jazz chord-melody style in C. At measure 31, I play a verse in more of a folk style, with arpeggiated accompaniment. I take another verse at measure 47. Beginning with measure 52, I introduce some new harmonies which lead to another key change. At measure 55, I'm once again in that great guitar key, D flat.

That's a *fermata*, or hold sign, in measure 58. Take a breath at the comma just before measure 61. Finally, be sure to hold on to the chord in measures 63 and 64 while you play the artificial harmonics.

About the recording...

I used the Kirk Sand nylon-string.

Amazing Grace

Words and Music by John Newton
Arranged by Craig B. Dobbins

© 1997 WARNER BROS. PUBLICATIONS U.S. INC.
All Rights Reserved

31

Leaning On The Everlasting Arms

Leaning, leaning, Safe and secure from all alarms;
Leaning, leaning, Leaning on the everlasting arms.

About the music...

Written in 1887 by Elisha A. Hoffman and Anthony J. Showalter. Corresponding by letter, Showalter wrote the text for the chorus, and Hoffman wrote the verses. Showalter then set the words to music.

Performance notes...

This arrangement is very much like *Since Jesus Came Into My Heart*, except that I begin with the chorus, rather than the verse.

The intro is played in classical style. At measure 5, it's thumbstyle (don't forget to mute the bass strings). I play a verse Carter-style at measure 40, with lots of hammers and pull-offs.

On the recording, the last time through the chorus, I slipped in an E7(#5) chord before going to the F. I finish the arrangement with a restatement of the intro at measure 59. That's an artificial harmonic at the end.

About the recording...

I used the Kirk Sand guitar, with just a little bit of echo from an old Boss delay unit.

Leaning On The Everlasting Arms

Words (Verses) by Elisha A. Hoffman

Words (Chorus) and Music by Anthony J. Showalter
Arranged by Craig B. Dobbins

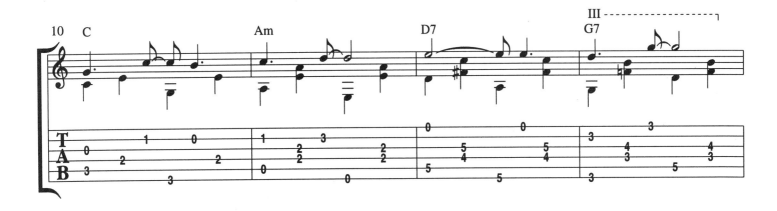

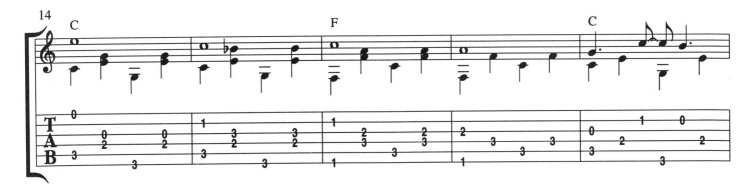

© 1997 WARNER BROS. PUBLICATIONS U.S. INC.
All Rights Reserved

34

In The Garden

*And the joy we share as we tarry there
None other has ever known.*

About the music...

This beloved hymn was composed by C. Austin Miles in 1912. He based the text on the passage from John 20, where Mary Magdalene meets the risen Jesus *in the garden*.

Performance notes...

My friend **Clyde Kendrick** kept telling me to unclutter the arrangement. "Don't be afraid to play a half note!" he advised, and it's true; sometimes you need to pause to let the music breathe.

Those are artificial harmonics played simultaneously with regular notes in measures 31 - 34.

Incidentally, **Paul Yandell** told me this is the first tune he learned to play as a youngster.

About the recording...

I used the Kirk Sand guitar.

In The Garden

Words and Music by C. Austin Miles
Arranged by Craig B. Dobbins

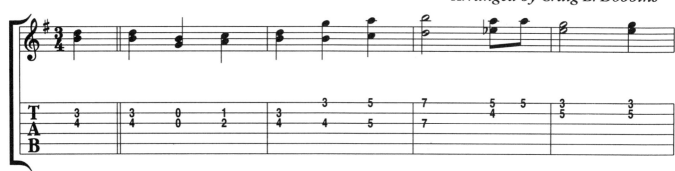

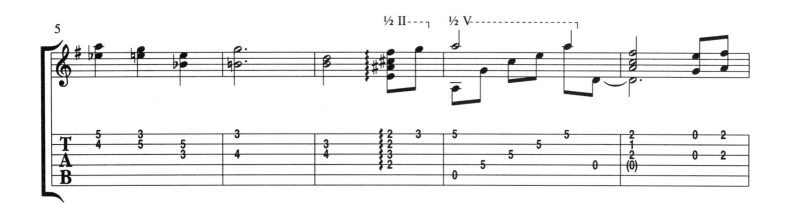

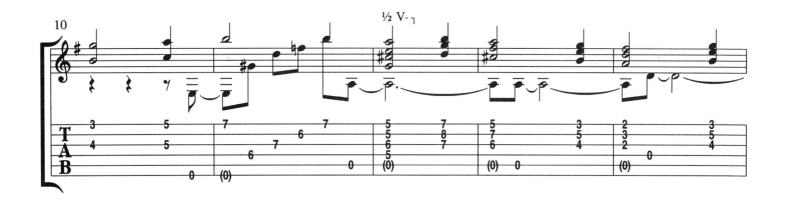

© 1997 WARNER BROS. PUBLICATIONS U.S. INC.
All Rights Reserved

38

Jesus, Keep Me Near The Cross

*Jesus, keep me near the cross, There a precious fountain
Free to all — a healing stream, Flows from Calvary's mountain.*

About the music...

In 1869, machinery manufacturer William H. Doane sent this melody to his friend Fanny J. Crosby, who wrote the text. The two also wrote *To God Be The Glory, Pass Me Not, O Gentle Savior, I Am Thine, O Lord* and *Rescue The Perishing*. Crosby wrote over *nine thousand* other hymn-poems, among them *Blessed Assurance, Jesus Is Mine*.

Performance notes...

This one's for my dad. It's just a simple country gospel arrangement, but (hopefully) with lots of feeling. I try to imagine **Paul Yandell's** playing on the old **Louvin Brothers** recordings from the 1950's.

The lead guitar stays close to the melody, occasionally playing two- or three-part harmonies. The grace notes are quick hammers or pull-offs. At the pickup to measure 33, I play the melody in the bass for a few measures.

The rhythm guitar plays a simple bass/strum/strum accompaniment throughout, then drops out at measure 65. I close with a few bars of fingerstyle.

About the recording...

That's the Kirk Sand guitar on lead, and the Martin on rhythm. I used a mike on the Martin, and recorded the Sand direct (as usual).

Jesus, Keep Me Near The Cross

Words by Fanny J. Crosby

Music by William H. Doane
Arranged by Craig B. Dobbins

© 1997 WARNER BROS. PUBLICATIONS U.S. INC.
All Rights Reserved

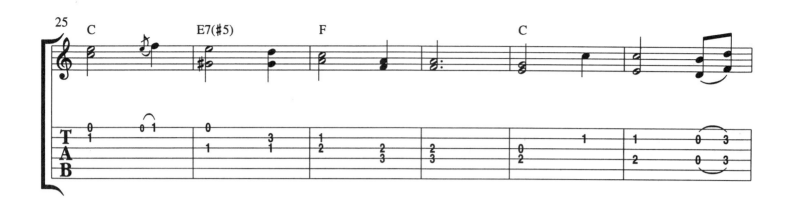

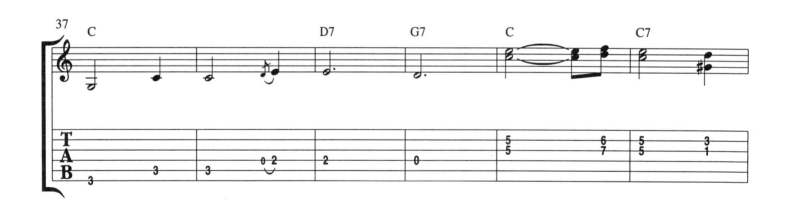
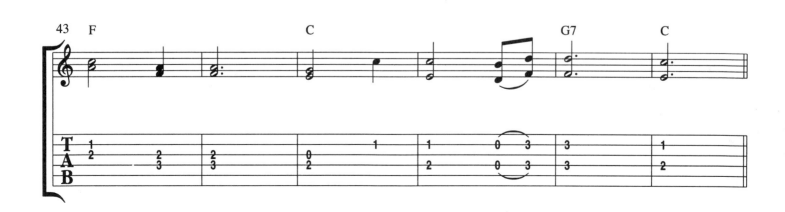

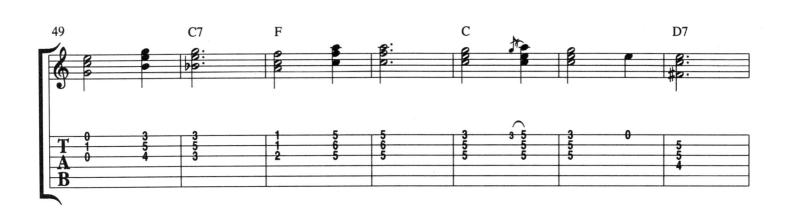
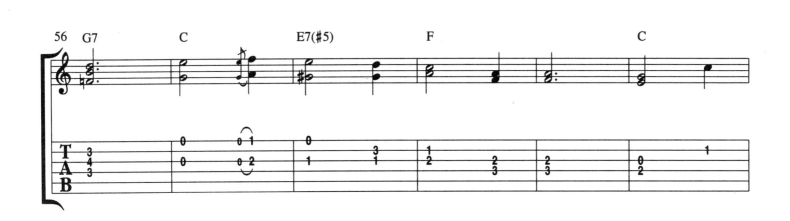
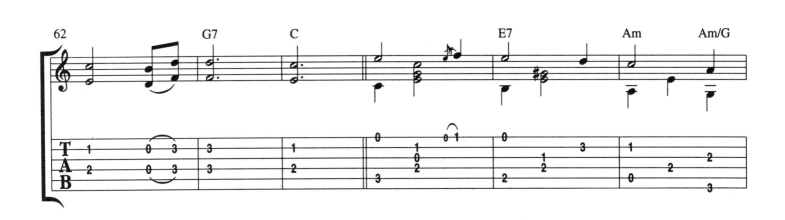

There Is A Fountain

Words by William Cowper

Music by Lowell Mason
Arranged by Craig B. Dobbins

© 1997 WARNER BROS. PUBLICATIONS U.S. INC.
All Rights Reserved

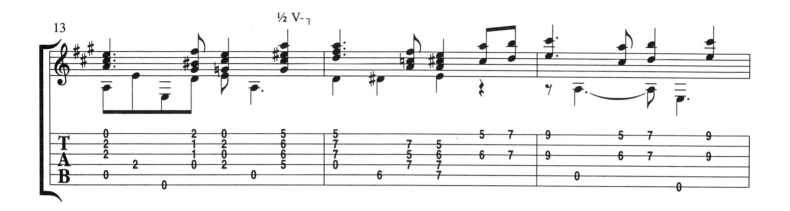
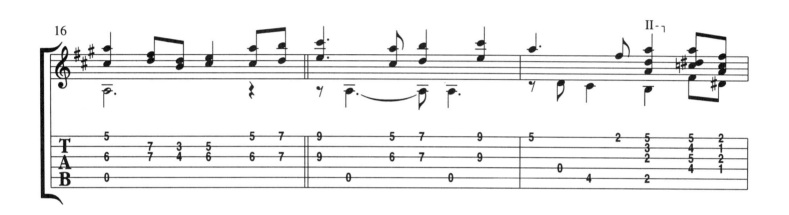

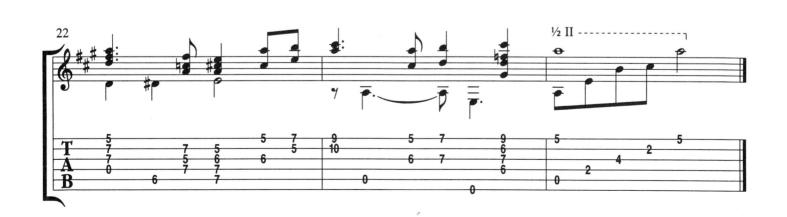

There Is A Fountain

*There is a fountain filled with blood drawn from Immanuel's veins;
And sinners, plunged beneath that flood, Lose all their guilty stains.*

About the music...

The English poet William Cowper, a friend of John Newton (author of *Amazing Grace*), wrote this hymn in 1771. The origin of the melody is unknown, but it was set to these words by Lowell Mason.

Performance notes...

This arrangement was inspired by versions I have heard church pianists play.

I begin with a single string melody in E. At the pickup to measure 9, I play stacked chords in the key of A.

About the recording...

I used the Kirk Sand guitar.

ACOUSTIC GUITAR TAB GLOSSARY

TABLATURE EXPLANATION

READING TABLATURE: Tablature illustrates the six strings of the guitar. Notes and chords are indicated by the placement of fret numbers on a given string(s).

String ⑥, 3rd Fret   String ① 12th Fret   A "C" Chord   C Chord Arpeggiated
String ② 13th Fret

HARMONICS

 **NATURAL HARMONIC:** A finger of the fret hand lightly touches the note or notes indicated in the tab and is played by the pick hand.

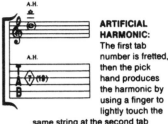 **ARTIFICIAL HARMONIC:** The first tab number is fretted, then the pick hand produces the harmonic by using a finger to lightly touch the same string at the second tab number (in parenthesis) and is then picked by another finger.

BENDING NOTES

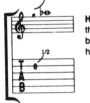 **HALF STEP:** Play the note and bend string one half step.*

 **PREBEND (Ghost Bend):** Bend to the specified note, before the string is picked.

 **WHOLE STEP:** Play the note and bend string one whole step.

 **PREBEND AND RELEASE:** Bend the string, play it, then release to the original note.

 **SLIGHT BEND (Microtone):** Play the note and bend string slightly to the equivalent of half a fret.

 **BENDS INVOLVING MORE THAN ONE STRING:** Play the note and bend string while playing an additional note (or notes) on another string(s). Upon release, relieve pressure from additional note(s), causing original note to sound alone.

 **DOUBLE NOTE BEND:** Play both notes and immediately bend both strings simultaneously.

 **BENDS INVOLVING STATIONARY NOTES:** Play notes and bend lower pitch, then hold until release begins (indicated at the point where line becomes solid).

ARTICULATIONS

 **HAMMER ON:** Play lower note, then "hammer on" to higher note with another finger. Only the first note is attacked.

 **PULL OFF:** Play higher note, then "pull off" to lower note with another finger. Only the first note is attacked.

 **LEFT HAND HAMMER:** Hammer on the first note played on each string with the left hand.

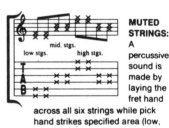 **MUTED STRINGS:** A percussive sound is made by laying the fret hand across all six strings while pick hand strikes specified area (low, mid, high strings).

FRET-BOARD TAPPING: "Tap" onto the note indicated by + with a finger of the pick hand, then pull off to the following note held by the fret hand.

© 1996 BELWIN-MILLS PUBLISHING CORP.
All Rights Administered by WARNER BROS. PUBLICATIONS U.S. INC.
All Rights Reserved including Public Performance for Profit

About the Author

Craig Dobbins lives in Gadsden, Alabama, with his wife Julie, and son Craig Bennett Jr. He is the author of THE GUITAR STYLE OF JERRY REED, and has written for FINGERSTYLE GUITAR magazine and MISTER GUITAR (journal of the Chet Atkins Appreciation Society). He also writes and publishes ACOUSTIC GUITAR WORKSHOP, a quarterly instructional package featuring written arrangements in notation and tab, with teaching comments and cassette.

Craig's recording FINGERPICKIN' GUITAR SOLOS and the matching transcription book are also available from ACOUSTIC GUITAR WORKSHOP.

For information, please write Craig c/o ACOUSTIC GUITAR WORKSHOP, P.O.Box 8075, Gadsden AL, 35902.